You Too Can Make Money In Voice Overs

An Easy To Understand Handbook For Complete Beginners

Sharon Brogden

YOU TOO CAN MAKE MONEY IN VOICE-OVERS

Copyright © 2010 Sharon Brogden

www.sharonbrogden.com / www.gbvcoltd.com

ISBN 978-1-4467-0323-6

Table of Contents

Acknowledgements

This book is dedicated to my daughter Olivia, without her, I would have still been working the 9-5 and earning just enough to pay the bills, but not enough to afford the luxuries.

I would also like to thank the global friends that I made in the internet chat room service PalTalk for recognising my talent and encouraging me to follow this career path.

My thanks also to my parents, Brian and Phyllis, for supporting me both financially and emotionally during the bad times and helping me along the way. Their continued support and encouragement is priceless.

Foreword

One of the first questions people interested in voice-over ask is, "do I have what it takes to make it?" A logical question, of course. It would seem as if "making it in voice-over" would depend upon a mysterious factor called talent, something you either have or you don't. But I think the entire concept of talent is a trap. If your mother thinks you have talent, do you? Probably not. If you think you have talent, do you? Also, debatable. If a casting director or producer thinks you sound great and hires you for a job, do you have talent then? Well, maybe. But then, if the next 20 people you approach for work hire someone else, what happened to your talent? Did it disappear?

Talent is not an external quality, as if the talented are winners of a vocal beauty contest. Talent is something you earn after years of developing and honing a craft, and after proving your worth to others by contributing to and supporting their efforts.

We cannot and should not let outside forces or anybody else's subjective judgment of ourselves determine whether or not we will be successful in life, or able to pursue a lifelong dream.

Nevertheless, there are some "success factors" that will determine whether or not the odds will be in your favor to become a working professional voice talent. Notice that voice quality and talent are not on the list.

VOICE TALENT SUCCCESS FACTORS

- Humility. No one is born knowing how to do voice-over. It's a learned skill.

- Willingness to listen and learn. You need an experienced set of outside ears to help point you in the right direction. We cannot be objective about ourselves.

- Marketing skills. Voice-over is show BUSINESS.

- Persistence. You could get work right away but you may have to send out many demos and make hundreds of phone calls before you book your first job.

- Great people skills. You must be likeable and fun to be around.

- Acting skills. The ability to get outside your head and portray other people's visions about characters, products and services using your voice.

- Reading skill. You must be able to read copy smoothly.

- Self starter. You can't rely on agents to get you work. They might help but they won't do it all. It's definitely possible to get work without an agent.

- A cool head. You can't freak out when you make the inevitable mistakes.

- Willingness to master a minimal set of technology skills to be able to record auditions from home.

- Some money to invest in training and basic home recording gear.

Bottom line:

YOU have to make the decision about whether or not voice-over is something you want to pursue. This is a competitive business and you will not get rich quick. (Although I am continually surprised at how well some of my beginning students are doing - several have told me recently of booking $2,000 jobs within their first few months in the business).

Anything that is lacking in your skill set can be fixed or learned, no matter what kind of voice you have. But what you cannot get from me or from anyone else is the desire, drive, and permission to allow yourself to pursue a lifelong goal.

Susan Berkley

Introduction

In the autumn of 2005, I was fired from my job because I was pregnant! Ridiculous, I know. We are supposed to be living in a time where people are treated equally. To cut a long story short, I sued the company for unfair dismissal and sex discrimination. I was awarded a substantial amount in compensation. However, the company went in to liquidation, and I didn't receive a penny.

So there I was, heavily pregnant, with very few prospects for the future. The bills were mounting up and I was slipping in to debt with a vengeance.

In March of 2006, I went in to labour during a serious asthma attack, which threatened the lives of both my baby and myself. After an emergency operation and after losing 4 pints of blood, Olivia arrived. We were both very poorly for some time afterwards, but with the help of family and a few very close friends, we eventually got back to a reasonable level of health.

During this time, I joined a family chat room on the internet, one of the many provided by Paltalk.com, and began chatting with people all over the world while Olivia slept.

It was one of those chat rooms where you actually speak over a microphone to the other chat room members, rather than just typing conversations on to the screen. It wasn't long before people started to comment on my voice and suggested that I should look in to doing voice-over work.

I had nothing to lose, I was an unemployed single mum, heavily in debt and, because my health wasn't completely back to normal, I had very few employment prospects. So I decided to make a few enquiries.

After several weeks of research using the library and the internet, I borrowed £300 from my family, enrolled on a voice-over workshop, and began making money from voice-over work.

A lot of money!

In April 2008 I started The Great British Voice Company, a brokerage service specialising in genuine British accent voice over artists. The company was such a huge success, that in September of 2009 I was awarded the 'Entrepreneur Of The Year' award at a regional business awards ceremony.

Back in 2006, I would never had imagined that I would be working again, let alone, working for myself, doing what I love and *earning more money in one day than most people earn in a week!*

This book aims to get you on the first rung of the voice-over ladder, without spending a fortune. In an easy to understand format. It aims to teach you how to get started, the skills required and how to develop them, how to set up a home studio on a budget, how to put together your voice over demo, how to market yourself as a voice talent, where to find your first voice over jobs, and much, much more. Basically, I'm going to show you how I did it.

So, if you're struggling to make ends meet, like I was, or just fancy enough money for a few extra luxuries, give voice-over a try, you'll wonder why you didn't do it sooner!

Chapter 1

What is a voice-over?

The most familiar voice-overs that you will have come across are the pictures on TV commercials and documentaries, which are often linked by a voice adding to the information we get from the pictures on the screen. This is a voice-over or a narration. It's called voice-over because it goes over the pictures. Often, either term is used.

Narration or voice-over is needed for many genres (kinds) of media content. We encounter voice-overs in so many contexts - in the cinema, on TV, on the radio etc. However voice talents are also needed for a large number of other tasks on different media platforms. It is easy to forget that professional voices are needed for things such as recorded messages at railway stations and airports, for announcements of platform numbers or gates, arrivals and departures, safety messages such as "Mind the Gap" or information about security policies.

A voice-over is also regularly used in lifts or elevators to announce floor numbers and safety messages. The voice telling you that the lift is "Going Up" is provided by a real person, i.e. a voice-over actor or voice talent.

Have you thought about the recorded guide for a museum, the voice giving directions on your GPS navigation system, or the voice on the apps that you have just downloaded for your iphone ® or ipad ®? These voices are all provided by real people known as voice-over artists, voice actors or voice talents.

Since the arrival of the internet, computerisation and new forms of media, there has been an explosion of work for the unseen vocal talent. Twenty years ago, computer games, e-learning and recorded telephone announcements didn't exist.

Here are a few examples of voice over work available, some of which, you may have not even considered.

In entertainment:

Movies for cinema release	Narration on Documentaries (which later can go to TV)
	Animation Character Voices (cartoons and long form dramas)
	Narration on Big Budget Documentaries (later going to TV)

T.V.	Commercials
	Station identification
	Program links and announcements
	Government public service announcements
	Program voice-overs e.g. documentaries
	Animation character voices (made for TV short cartoons and program length stories.
Radio	Radio commercials and jingles
	Program links and announcements
	Government public service announcements
	Station identification
	Program presentation e.g. D.J's, arts, religion
Computer & video games	Character voices & narration

Instructions and help

Impersonations	Celebrity and political figures for commercials, conferences etc.
Funfairs	Entertainment rides and puppet shows

Education & public service field:

CD's, DVD's, video, internet,	Audio books, guided meditation, relaxation and hypnosis
	Talking blogs
	Exercise videos
	Educational material and tutorials - science, maths, geography etc.
Ipod or mp3 players	Museum & art gallery portable guides, audio tours

In business & professional contexts:

CD Roms, DVD's, videos, podcasts, e-learning & internet

Corporate promotional videos

Educational products e.g. sales techniques or medical subjects,

Business presentations for conferences and exhibitions

Website video voice-overs

Set up and software tutorials

Voicemail, on-hold messaging, interactive voice response (IVR)

GPS navigation

Podcast introductions

Smart phone applications

Rail and airport & in flight safety and service announcements

Lifts

Foreign languages

For all media platforms   Dubbing of character voices and
narration for drama or documentary.

A special note about news and current affairs: These kinds
of programs on TV and radio use voice over a lot, but the
voices are usually those of journalists and not general vocal
talents. In drama and animation often celebrity or known
actors are used, sometimes voice talents.

Chapter 2

Basic requirements

What do you need to get started in voice-over? Well a voice of course – but what sort of sound? Until the late 1960's the only voices that were heard on radio and TV were well modulated "proper" professional voices. Everyone sounded like middle class bank managers! The arrival of the Beatles was a change-maker. In interviews the difference was striking, between the stuffy sounding media and the natural, lively "Fab Four", who sounded real with their Liverpool accents.

Since then radio and TV has featured a wide variety of accents and tones. Media managers want voices that sound like someone you know, but are interesting – a little offbeat and individual is even better. Voices that are distinctive but not distinguished, are in great demand. In the major centres like London, New York or Los Angeles, your "one-off" voice would probably earn you enough work to keep your bank balance healthy.

Outside the big cities the amount of work is less, and therefore there is less demand for an unusual voice. To be successful you need to be versatile so you can be considered for different types of voice work. If your voice is free of an accent that identifies a region or social class and is easy on the ear - the chances are you will be hired more often.

Having experience in the media helps. There was a time when the usual background for freelance voice artists was acting, reading the news or presenting TV and Radio programs. However sometimes you have to "unlearn" some of that experience. Radio DJ's (disc jockeys) who give the upbeat intros to popular hits *can* make it as freelancers but these kinds of programs have a particular style. Ex DJ's often have to practice speaking normally, as if they were chatting in your kitchen, and drop the over enthusiastic energy that was part of their former job.

No matter what sort of voice you have, there are basic professional skills that you must develop in order to make it in the marketplace.

For many of us, we began to think about working professionally as a voice artist because enough people had remarked that we "sounded good on the phone" and had a voice that was nice to hear. Compliments like these, and a lot of ambition, triggered my exploring this field, although I had no background in broadcast media. I became a sought after voice artist because I learnt along the way, that having a nice voice isn't enough. For example a flat read of a piece of copy (script), isn't interesting to listen to and you are unlikely to be hired very often. It is essential to have some basic acting skills as well as a good instrument, your voice. Like all instruments, it needs tuning.

Chapter 3

Care of your voice

Your vocal instrument – your voice - must be looked after. Like the rest of the body, that means exercise. Producing sound involves many parts. Sound begins in the chest, so the chest muscles and the diaphragm need exercise. (The diaphragm is the muscle that stretches across the top of your stomach under your lungs). Your vocal cords in your throat mustn't be sore from a cough or cold, and need to be kept supple. Lastly the mouth – lips, tongue, and the jaw muscles shape the sound. Together they form the vowel sounds (a, e, i, o and u), and enunciate the consonants (t, d, l, m, s, p, g etc.).

It pays to do vocal exercises every day. I do mine in the car or in front of a mirror, especially before recording sessions, so my vocal instrument is warm and flexible before I begin recording, or when I get to the studio.

Tongue twisters are an excellent way to exercise the voice and warm up the muscles of the jaw and vocal cords. Here are some tongue twisters that you may be familiar with - try them at different speeds:

Red leather, yellow leather.

A proper cup of coffee in a copper coffeepot.

Better buy the bigger brighter rubber baby buggy bumpers.

Lips teeth tip of the tongue.

Tim told Todd today to take two tiny tablets tomorrow.

Peter Piper picked a peck of pickled peppers.

Did Peter Piper pick a peck of pickled peppers?

If Peter Piper picked a peck of pickled peppers

Where's the peck of pickled peppers Peter Piper picked?

Practice with different exercises, or make up some of your own, especially if there are any sounds which you have trouble with.

Breath is the foundation of voice work so you need to exercise your diaphragm and chest muscles as well. Take deep breaths. Inhale through your nose and fill your chest, your tummy will expand too, then exhale through your nose, letting the air out slowly, and gradually contract your stomach muscles. Do this several times and then repeat it, but inhale and exhale though your mouth.

Next, an exercise familiar to all vocal performers - inhale through your nose, fill your chest and then say "ahhh" as you exhale, keep it going for the duration of your out breath, pull your stomach muscles in and keep going until your chest is empty. Do several repeats, and then do the same exercise but inhale air though your mouth.

You can check if your diaphragm is getting stronger by repeating these words in one breath as many times as you can:-

Harriet Hubbard helps her husband, Henry Hubbard, hose his dirty caravan down.

This exercise is great for breath control and articulation – start slowly, and repeat it again and again, getting faster:-

On one breath –

Buh Duh Guh Duh
Buh Duh Guh Duh
Buh Duh Guh Duh
Buh Duh Guh Duh
Buh Duh Guh Duh
Buh Duh Guh Duh

Then

Guh Duh Buh Duh
Guh Duh Buh Duh
Guh Duh Buh Duh
Guh Duh Buh Duh
Guh Duh Buh Duh
Guh Duh Buh Duh

Now

Puh Tuh Kuh Tuh
Puh Tuh Kuh Tuh
Puh Tuh Kuh Tuh
Puh Tuh Kuh Tuh
Puh Tuh Kuh Tuh
Puh Tuh Kuh Tuh

Then

Kuh Tuh Puh Tuh
Kuh Tuh Puh Tuh
Kuh Tuh Puh Tuh
Kuh Tuh Puh Tuh
Kuh Tuh Puh Tuh
Kuh Tuh Puh Tuh

Thanks to Melanie Haynes for that one. More about Melanie can be found on her website MelanieHaynes.com.

It is not just a matter of your voice and lungs being in good condition, to be a professional, your entire body must be in reasonably good shape for work. I know from experience that you need stamina to concentrate and read copy in a studio all day. If you tire easily it will be noticeable in your voice performance. A tired performer stumbles and makes more mistakes. Your normal exercise routine will help your cardio-vascular system perform well. Add stomach exercises – "sit ups", as they will strengthen your stomach muscles. You must get in shape. It makes working with your voice all day less effort.

Your energy levels are important for another reason. Even in a straight read, a sense of vitality and energy are present in the voice. The listener gains a sense of a live person – a personality - even if they cannot see them. This is even more so when you are required to play a character. The character will not seem real if there is no energy and life behind the voice.

Yet oddly, too much energy in the form of tension is also detectable. The voice can be a little "tight" or strangled, and can sound a bit anxious under the stress of performance on cue, so all actors and vocal performers do relaxation exercises before "the play begins". These exercises will help your body and mind relax but still be alertly ready so you can pitch your energy correctly for the job.

Yawn! – Yes – breathe in deeply and yawn at the same time. Stretch your mouth and face muscles with a really big yawn, and tighten your neck and shoulder muscles. Then sigh as you let the air out gradually. Relax any tension that is present in your shoulders, arms, neck and face. Do it slowly. Do several and you will find it very relaxing.

Stick your tongue out!: Try to make it touch the tip of your nose, and then the bottom of your chin. This exercise helps your tongue be flexible, especially if the job calls for some multi-syllable words or tricky phrases. Perhaps face a wall so no one takes offence!

Scrunch your face! Your face needs to be relaxed yet responsive too. Your facial expression can affect the sound of your voice. Can there be a smile in your voice if your face is frowning? Open your mouth as wide as you absolutely can. Then scrunch up your face – tighten your cheeks, lips, eyes and forehead and clench your teeth as if you were about to move a boulder. Now add your entire body – fists, arms, neck, shoulders – you have to move that boulder up a hill. Count to ten – then relax. Try it a few times, feel how relaxing it is?

Watch what you eat

Believe it or not, the food that you eat prior to a recording session can either help or hinder your vocal performance.

When you begin speaking in to the microphone, you should be using your diaphragm to help with your breath control, if you eat certain foods it can make it harder to take in full breaths.

Certain foods can also cause a lot of mucus to build up in the throat, which sounds dreadful when picked up on your recordings.

I'm not asking you to starve yourself. If possible, you should eat a light meal approximately two hours before a voice-over session. It is important to eat to keep up your strength, just be careful what you *do* eat.

Before a recording session you should eat a light meal and stay away from stodgy or heavy foods that can interfere with your breathing techniques. You should also avoid dairy products such as milk and cheese as they are the main culprit for causing mucus to build up in the back of your mouth and throat, making it harder to breathe correctly and causing excess mouth noise.

Whether you are just putting together a demo, auditioning for a job or recording a paid voice-over, it is important to watch what you eat.

You should also drink lots of water to keep yourself and your vocal cords well hydrated. It's a good idea to have a bottle of fresh water in your studio, long form narration such as audio books, can really dry out your mouth and this will be evident on the finished recording.

Caffeinated drinks such as tea and coffee should be avoided for at least two hours prior to recording, because they will also dry out your mouth and contribute to that unwanted mouth noise. Carbonated drinks such as fizzy pop, fizzy water or soda, should also be avoided because they produce excess gas in your stomach making it difficult to maintain a consistent pace or pitch.

Avoid alcohol for at least 12 hours prior to recording. It's a known fact that alcohol can be very dehydrating, not only to the body but also to the vocal cords

Citrus fruits (oranges, grapefruit, pineapple etc.) should be avoided too, as they have the same drying out effect as coffee and tea.

Drinks should be lukewarm or at least, not straight from the cooler as the cold will cause your throat to constrict and you will get the temptation to swallow in order to relieve the tightness.

Foods that are ideal include chicken, fish, eggs, salads and rice. Lukewarm drinks can help soothe your throat before a vocal performance. Salt water and honey can also help your throat. Watch what you are eating and drinking, this will help bring out your natural vocal talent.

A top tip to help eliminate any excess mouth noise that you may be experiencing is to eat a Granny Smiths apple, so keep a supply in your store cupboard.

If you smoke – STOP! We are all aware of the serious health complications that smoking can cause. It also irritates the throat and vocal cords causing your voice to sound hoarse. Not only that, it reduces your lung capacity and makes breathing difficult.

Chapter 4

Developing your skills

A voice talent must be able to read a script and understand its content. This understanding is important because a flat read – in a routine monotone - isn't interesting to listen to and usually fails to communicate the meaning of the text. A voice must have expression – but not too much. A read that is too sugary or too "hammy" is "on the nose" or "cheesy", unless of course the material (and the producer/director) calls for that over-the-top-style. You need good judgment to know how the copy should be voiced and depending on the job – some acting skills. It is a performance but for voice only.

Finding your best voice

It may sound strange but speaking naturally when stood in front of a microphone, reading from a script, is not easy, it takes practice, and lots of it. Without practice, it will be obvious that you are reading from a script and it won't sound natural at all. A huge amount of voice-over jobs advertised these days have a requirement for a conversational tone, as if the voice artist is just chatting to a friend. When you're reading from a script, sounding conversational can be extremely difficult at first. This skill takes time to develop.

Try these exercises to help you sound more natural. Vary your pitch patterns (high and low voice), vary the pace (speed), don't worry about making sense as you do this, just put as much variation in to each text as you possibly can. Repeat each exercise four of five times, with a different variation each time.

1. *Never, oh, never, the fatal endeavour, the ties that they sever, the fatal endeavour.*

2. *Were it far or near or nearer and nearer*

3. *The incredible, edible, sheddable, beddable, blinking, twinkling, nodding, prodding, pointed, icicle popsicle.*

4. *How could you? How would you? How did you? How might you? How may you? How can you? How dare you?*

5. *Other than that or this or those, might one not speak of a bright red rose.*

Another good exercise to help you develop a more natural, conversational tone is to take a passage from a book and read it out loud in a monotone (all on one note), then repeat the same passage a note higher, and again a note higher, continue until you have reached the highest note that you can comfortably read at, without straining your vocal cords. Be careful not to sing!

Repeat this exercise in your normal monotone voice, but this time, go down the scale. Stop when it gets uncomfortable.

Lastly, read the text out loud as you would normally do so, you will find that pitch and pace will begin to vary naturally.

Practice this exercise as often as you can, two or three times a day if possible. This will help to develop a broad vocal range so that you are not uncomfortable reading text in varying pitches. Eventually varying your pitch when reading aloud will become second nature, and you won't even have to think about which pitch to use. You will automatically sound more natural and more conversational.

Read copy skilfully

The same applies for a straightforward read. You need to understand its meaning as well as any instructions you are given by the person who hires you, as to what sort of read they want. Often, all that is asked is to read it so that it sounds natural. However, even that can be a challenge. Sometimes a script for a voice over is written to be spoken in conversational English and with care for how it will be spoken, but it is not uncommon to be presented with a script that is the exact opposite. The sentence structure may be in formal written English with awkward phrasing.

The solution is to allow time to read it through – even study it. You need to find the natural breath points and give it a rhythm that works – that makes it sound real.

How do you locate these "breath points"? You need to think in terms of thoughts. When we chat we say something and then "um" and "err" or we say "well" and "like" – these are called fillers, which come in between thoughts while we think of the next point we want to make.

So speech is made up of groups of words that express a thought, sometimes they are called "thought groups". If the emphasis on words in the sentences and your intake of breaths are in the wrong places, the meaning of the text won't be clear. So you need to do practice reads of the copy in a conversational manner. You will find you pause naturally. These pauses and intakes of breath should occur where the punctuation is, but sometimes copy is badly written and there may be no punctuation where there should be. Sometimes the text is complex, for instance if it is on a medical, scientific or academic subject, with long complex sentences. It hasn't been written to be spoken aloud.

So, as you do your practice reads, notice where you pause naturally, and make a pencil mark – a slash - to indicate a pause. It may be different from the writer's punctuation. Two or three slashes means an extra beat, for instance at the start of a new paragraph. You will pause naturally after each group of words that complete a thought. Don't worry about perfect diction or possible errors as you do a practice read.

This basic technique is useful for all types of copy, including less natural voice-overs, such as hard-sell commercials that need to be spoken with speed and energy.

Imagining that you are just speaking to someone, (but not in a boring way), can help to prevent you projecting your voice too much. You are aiming to communicate the sense that you are in the room with the listener and they know you. It should not sound as if you are speaking from a pulpit or making an announcement.

If you read copy with an awareness of groups of words, each group communicating a meaningful thought, then your reads will be smoother with the intake of breaths in the right places.

How do you develop this skill?

Listen to radio and TV and be critical. Notice when something has been said badly. This will be difficult at first, as we are conditioned to believe that those people are professionals, so it must be right. It's not always the case. The more closely you listen, the more errors you will find.

Read and focus on whether you have understood what you are reading. Notice how it can be made meaningless if you read it with different pausing and stressing different words.

When you speak or answer the phone, practice putting a "smile in your voice" by thinking of your listener and wishing them well. Your voice will feel and sound much warmer.

As in all things – Practice makes a big difference!

Chapter 5

What to specialise in

Consider specialising in one or two different areas of the industry. This helps voice talents and voice recording studios market themselves. They make demo recordings which are available to potential clients. Having a sample that is in a style appropriate for particular tasks or sections of the industry, helps clients find what they are looking for - and hire them.

For example, someone with a good voice for documentary narration will make a demo reading a section from a documentary script. Then they ensure that recording studios that frequently do the sound mix for documentaries for film or TV, are aware of them and have a copy, along with their voice agent and as many documentary producers as possible.

The list in Chapter One gives an overview of the many sectors in the industry; it is worth considering which sectors your voice would naturally suit and then marketing your talent to them.

Narrating audio books

Books for the Blind have been around for a long time, and today many more people are living longer so there are more people whose eyesight becomes weaker in advanced old age. In addition, many people today are time poor and don't have time to read leisurely, yet most cars have CD and mp3 players, so listening to a narrated book as they drive, provides a change from music.

Apart from the classics, the latest fiction bestsellers – crime, romance and science fiction - are popular, so are nonfiction, self help topics such as relaxation and motivation. There are skills topics that sell well, such as sales or business negotiation.

A popular part of the non-fiction genre is biography, particularly celebrities and politicians. Parents are also keen buyers of audio books for children. Car journeys are much quieter with an entertaining story playing!

This sector of the industry has grown by almost 12% last year, which is expected to continue. Today this sector is approximately 17% of the industry and worth over £1 billion per year.

It is easy to find audio books in libraries and bookstores. Some companies provide magazines and daily newspapers as an audio version too.

Narrating museum and art gallery guides, educational documentaries.

The subject you narrate may be Elizabethan shipbuilding for The Maritime Museum, or the story of Leonardo Da Vinci's life for an art gallery. It could be Air Ships for a TV documentary. The delivery medium varies. It may be produced on CD Rom, DVD, tape, videotape, internet download, or multimedia – sound with timed images- a device often seen in museums.

If you think for a minute you can gauge the size of the market from your own experience.

Voice acting for cartoon films, talking toys, children's books, video games, etc.

NOTE- People often use two terms for voices in this field "Character Voice" and "Animated Voice". Usually by character voice they mean a voice that is like that of a real person – perhaps with an accent or dialect. Animation voice is the description often used for an unreal character – like a talking duck or train in a cartoon or a toy.

Corporate (business and industry) product:

This is another large area of demand for voices. There are sales videos, CD's, internet presentations and product promotions. Trade shows often have videos on their exhibition stands. Conferences may begin with a special motivational speech or a product launch. This sector also always needs training material on management, occupational health and safety, legal changes etc. This area of the industry overlaps with the education sector and with medical material.

Education & training: delivered on-line, or via DVD, CD Rom, or videotape.

Lifelong learning has been promoted since the year 2000. It is a field which is expanding for self-help programs, on-line tutorials, internet college classes, narrated textbooks, children's education films, adult continuing education training programs; the demand for all these is increasing.

Internet Specific Sector.

The arrival of the internet and the presence of a computer in every home, has made this area the fastest growing. It is at least 35% to 40% of most voice production work today. The Internet carries all the recognised types of material – educational and industrial, but it is also the medium for some less well known voice over products. Unless it is pointed out, it is easy to forget interactive guides to museums and universities and downloadable audio tours, flash presentations, spoken banner ads, podcasts, company promos and presentations about themselves and their products.

Medical and pharmaceutical material.

This industry sector needs voices for all the same products as other businesses, including medical training and the promoting of products and companies, but in addition, the medical field requires voice over for procedures to demonstrate surgical techniques and the use of new equipment that can be quite complicated. A voice-over talent may have to pronounce medical and chemical terms that are unfamiliar.

Film dubbing, ADR, looping: movies, television, video games, games for consoles.

Dubbing, looping and ADR (automated dialogue replacement), refer to the same thing. Dubbing is the practice of replacing sound shot on location with a re-recorded actor's voice in a recording studio. It may be replaced with the lines said in a different language, or because the sound was bad, (e.g. due to the sound of an aircraft) or to change the performance. The actor watches a sequence of shots, repeats the line and tries to match their lip movements to those on screen.

ADR is the modern digital method of matching re-recorded voice and existing pictures with numbers through a computer. Looping is the old method - by making a loop of the sequence of shots and playing it continuously until the actor managed to mimic the performance and mouth movements.

Voice talents don't usually replace actors in a major movie, except when a voice capable of speaking a foreign language is needed for dubbing and for sales to other markets.

Voice talents are used much more for video and console games. The new generations are like films with animated characters and narrators.

Telephony: menu prompts, IVR, information on hold, auto attendant, etc.

We are all familiar with the recorded messages on telephones. This recorded voice is called telephony. Companies take care in choosing a professional voice to project a certain image for their business and are likely to come back to the same voice artist when the system needs updating.

Just to remind you of how much work this can mean there are several scenarios:

Some systems prompt the caller through several choices. These are called "Menu Prompt" systems. The voice artist records dialogue such as "Please press 1 for credit cards, 2 for customer service, 3 for ..." The caller is then diverted to the appropriate department, where they may hear another voice over informing them that their "call is in a queue" and "thank you for holding, your call will be answered shortly".

Another area of telephony frequently encountered is an IVR (Interactive Voice Response) system. This allows the caller to speak to an automatic pre-recorded voice and a computer recognises their words. For example it is frequently used for taxi bookings. The IVR voice will say "Please say "Yes, No or Later" "Are you ready now?" or "Sorry, I didn't catch that, please repeat...". IVR systems are becoming much more common.

We are all familiar with voice mail – the message you hear when someone cannot take your call, and giving you the option of leaving a message or being transferred. Some companies refer to it as an "Auto Attendant System". It is so commonplace that providing the voice for the message is a good source of work. So is the message you so often hear whilst you are on hold waiting for a customer service officer to respond to your call. It often begins with "Your call is important to us, you have progressed in the queue." Or the voice enticingly offers you a product upgrade before saying "Your call will be answered very soon". This is called information on hold.

Chapter 6
Your home studio

Traditionally a voice over artist would be with an agency, would be booked and would then travel to a recording studio where there would be a permanently set up sound booth. The walls would be made of suitable sound absorbing material to prevent traffic noise or a slammed door from penetrating the sound booth. A good quality microphone would already be set up maybe in front of a chair.

In the last decade technology has revolutionised the options. You can be booked through the internet as an independent; the script can be sent the same way, usually by email. You can record the voice over in your home studio, perform any necessary editing yourself using the resources described later in this chapter, and send it back to the client via the internet.

Taking this option can be daunting when you don't know where to start with setting up a home studio and choosing a quality microphone. Here is an outline of the basics you need to know.

Do you have space for a small studio?

Consider your home; is there a corner, an alcove or a walk in cupboard spare? At its simplest you need space for a laptop or personal computer on a table, connected to a microphone on a stand. You can achieve this with a modest cash outlay.

You can of course spend a lot more and build a special soundproofed room with an expensive microphone, speakers and sound mixing equipment. But a basic set-up will usually be adequate to start with.

Can you make the space reasonably sound proof?

The first essential is quiet and plenty of it, in long periods. Perhaps you don't need to build sound proof walls; you may have a walk in wardrobe – a room within a room. Sit in the area you are thinking of using at different times of the day. Can you hear birds or distant traffic rumble? Is there the sound of water gurgling down a pipe or a washing machine audible?

You can install sound proofing, but be careful, it needs to be done using professional materials, not some foam or fiberglass product suggested by a friend of a friend. Quite often the techniques that sound recordists use on location may be sufficient. They hang blankets or heavy curtains to cut down on exterior sound. This is reasonably effective though some sound will still get through – but this you would probably be able to deal with through editing.

What is the basic equipment?

Most computers purchased are PC's with Windows. So these instructions are for them not Apple computers.

A fairly recent computer up to three years old, running Windows XP should be adequate. You need a good microphone, (I need to stress here, that most in-built microphones are not sufficient to use for voice over recording, you will need to invest a small amount in a decent quality studio microphone in order to produce a professional result), and software programs for recording and editing your sound. You can then save it as an MP3 file.

Basic equipment :

Personal Computer or lap-top

Intel Pentium 4 or equivalent processor

Windows 2000 or later / Windows XP / Vista

1 GB of available disk space

512 MB of RAM

Audio line in and Audio line out

USB studio condenser microphone (the Samson CO1U is good)

Full cover, noise eliminating headphones

Desktop speakers (in the voice industry, these are called monitors)

Recording and editing software (Audacity and NCH Wavepad are excellent, and, for the most part, they are free!).

Buying a Microphone

There is a studio condenser microphone that is robust and reliable - The Samson CO1U USB. It connects directly to your PC via a USB port; you don't need a mixing desk. The cost is reasonable, and it can be purchased for about £50. It is worth checking the internet and ebay for deals.

Choosing the software.

You need a software program which will record and edit audio. There are two programs which I recommend: Audacity and NCH Wavepad. Audacity is free and reliable. It is available for Windows, Mac OS X, GNU/ Linux, and other operating systems from these links.

Free Audacity Download :
http://audacity.sourceforge.net/download/

Audacity tutorials:
http://www.transom.org/tools/editing_mixing/200404.audacity.html

And: http://www.scribd.com/doc/8463893/How-to-Use-Audacity-Guide

You can use this program to record your voice, to convert tapes and records into digital format, and record onto formats such as CD's, save it as MP3, Ogg, Vorbis or WAV sound files. Also you can mix sound together and edit it, cut and splice tracks as well as change the speed and pitch of the sound.

NCH Wavepad can be downloaded from http://www.nch.com.au/wavepad/masters.html.

This is a basic trial version, the full version costs about £45 which is a modest sum for most.

This program is the easiest editing tool to use. It performs edits and you can convert sound from one format to another e.g. WAV format to MP3, aiff etc. and vice versa.

NCH Wavepad tutorial:
http://www.webjam.com/alcelearning/wavepad_tutorial

This is a simple tutorial with good diagrams.

All these downloadable tutorials explain the basics of how to record sound. The Audacity tutorial also includes more complicated projects to try when you become confident.

The total cost of your equipment and software is not much more than £100 as long as you have a PC.

Chapter 7

Recording and editing

The software instructions for Audacity and NCH Wavepad are easy to follow but there is no substitute for unhurried practical experience.

Record yourself reading any text from a newspaper or magazine and edit out errors, breaths, hisses and extraneous sounds, don't worry, the majority of this can be done by highlighting the area of the recording that you want to remove, just by clicking with the mouse, dragging across and pressing the delete key.

If you need to add a pause in to your recording, this can be done easily by clicking 'Edit' and then 'insert slience'. Wavepad uses MS (Milliseconds), so 500 MS would be half a second.

Most background hiss can also be removed by using the 'Noise Reduction' tool in Wavepad. Don't forget to remove the unwanted silence at the beginning and end of the recording by dragging across it with your mouse and pressing the delete key. An acceptable silence before the voice starts and after the voice ends, is around one second, so remove any excess. Follow the tutorials for detailed step by step guides.

Do this enough times to feel confident before you take on your first voice-over commission. It's not fun to learn something under the pressure of a deadline.

Even then you must allow more time. Beginners usually need to double or triple the time that experienced voice over talents take. The rule of thumb is that editing and producing the final copy takes at least an extra 100% of the time it took to record the job.

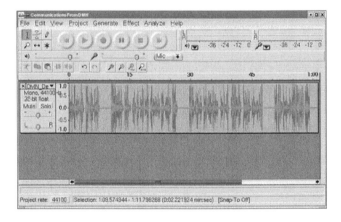

Recording with Audacity

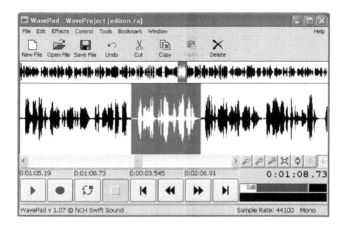

Editing with NCH Wavepad

My first commission was a three minute voice over for a trade show exhibition stand video. I recorded the copy several times until I was happy with the tone and pacing, then I edited out the blemishes, such as the sound of background hiss and breaths, which took about 40 minutes. So all in all, it took about one hour. Today the same job would take me ten minutes. It is just practice.

Of course if you are attending one of my workshops for beginners, you will receive a good basic practical grounding in how to use both these types of software, and the reassurance of having someone to hand who can answer questions.

Chapter 8

Creating your demo

To obtain work you need to promote yourself. To do this you need to produce a sample of what you sound like, for potential clients to hear. This is called a voice-over demo or voice-reel. They used to be on cassette tape, now they are produced on CD and made available on the internet as mp3 files.

A client looking for a suitable voice can go to your website or the website of a voice agent, click on a picture of the voice talent with a few lines of biography beside it, and then click to hear their voice.

A voice demo is sometimes also called a showreel, though that term originally referred to a video or CD of scenes showing a screen actor's best performances.

You need a demo or CD which shows the different styles of voice-over you are offering. You need to think carefully about what you do best.

People usually begin with a demo of four or five different styles. If you are very versatile and perhaps can offer another language, then consider creating more than one demo CD or voice-reel if you need to target very different sectors of the industry.

How long should it be?

A demo can be as short as thirty seconds, or as long as three minutes. Clients are busy, so a demo between 1.30 to 2.00 minutes for a CD is a good length to give a sense of your voice without overdoing it. A demo intended to be heard over the internet should be shorter most are 1.00 minute to 1.30 minutes, and the file is 1MB or just over. This size can be downloaded quickly and easily and without losing any audio quality.

It's not a good idea to record your first demo yourself unless you are competent with adding music and sound effects. Your demo needs to sound fantastic! After all, it's the single most important marketing tool that you have, and if it sounds mediocre or homemade, a client will be less than impressed, and it won't get you much work.

To begin with, have your demo made professionally. The Great British Voice Company (www.greatbritishvoice.co.uk) can produce a professional demo including background music and sound effects, at a reasonable price. Contact them for details.

How should the content be organised?

All clients are familiar with the way a radio program flows, so a demo usually follows the same pattern, with very brief snatches of music and announcements between each style sample. It is usual to offer five or six reads, with different content, pace, and vocal tone.

The breaks between each read are often called bumpers or sweepers. They consist of a few bars of music, often called a jingle or music bed and an identification (a voice very briefly saying what you are about to hear). A break without music but with a voice is called an "ID", a stager or a sweep.

At the beginning you would identify yourself and perhaps the type of work your voice samples are pitched at. For example: "John Smith. Voice Demo – Audio Books. Above all don't drag it out, keep it crisp and moving.

A Sample Demo:

Intro: .05   sec – Give your name, and content area

Segment 1:   .15

Segment 2:   .15

Segment 3:   .10

Segment 4:   .10

Segment 5:   .05

Close: .05   - Contact Phone No/ Website Address

Music jingle: .05 – 08 - Optional

If you are sending out CD's make sure the exterior of the case and the CD itself are identified clearly with your name and contact details. CD's often become orphans and busy people will just throw it out rather than listen to it all the way through to find out what is on the CD. Also it saves a possible client having to load the CD again to listen to your contact details.

Chapter 9
Marketing yourself

Working freelance

As you are just starting out as a new voice-over talent, the best way to get your first few jobs, is by working freelance, that is, without the help of an agent. Very few agents will take on a voice that is completely new to the industry, unless they can demonstrate remarkable talent right from the start. It will be difficult for them to pitch your voice to customers against the more experienced talent that they already have on their books.

My advice is to start as a freelance voice talent. There are several places where you can find work as a freelancer, detailed later in this chapter.

However, there are some drawbacks to working freelance, the main one being that you probably won't be hired for a high budget production. The majority of work that you will find as a freelancer will be lower budget work for telephone system recordings, short corporate videos, website introductions etc. It may not pay for your next vacation, but it will put some much needed extra cash in to your bank account. For example, a 30 second telephone recording may earn you in the region of £30 to £50. Bearing in mind that, as a beginner, it could take up to an hour to complete, it's still pretty decent money when compared to the average salary per hour in the usual 9 -5 job. A couple of these a week in your spare time, can drastically improve your finances within a few weeks.

The main advantage of finding voice-over work as a freelancer is that you usually get to keep all the money you earn instead of your agent taking a cut.

Should you find an agent?

Joining a voice-over talent agency is a usually a good idea, as soon as you have some experience and are comfortable with the recording and editing process. It's essential in the larger cities. Some are active agents, who will put forward your voice for auditions and promote you, others simply have a website with a list of their talent and samples of their work but that is all. A few set up a web page for each voice over talent, with the opportunity to upload many audio samples of work and some with video too. Most take a percentage commission from all jobs; others charge a flat fee for listing you. Current legislation regards any upfront fees charged by an agent just for listing you, as unethical. The industry standard and internationally recognised format, is to take a commission from each voice job that you are selected for, with no upfront listing fees.

Voice-over market places or listing sites, do usually charge a registration fee, but this is because they are not classified as an agent, and do not take any commission from the money you earn through that particular site. The current fee for an online presence in a voice marketplace is around £200 a year, but many charge far less. More about voice-over marketplaces later in this chapter.

It is also hard to say whether going with a large agency or an expensive one will bring you more work. If they have many talents, and you are a new unknown voice, your name may not be mentioned or put forward for auditions very often.

Yet the opposite is no guarantee of work either. A small agency with fewer names may not be as well connected with casting directors or commercial producers at advertising agencies. When there is work available, smaller agencies may not receive a phone call asking about the voices listed with them.

How then do you choose? As you make contact with an agent, evaluate how you are treated. Is there a friendly professional attitude? Are calls returned? It may give you some insight regarding how they would handle inquiries from producers. If you can, talk to other voice talents about their opinions of agents. However you cannot judge from the amount of work they say they get through an agent - your talents and experience might be different.

As in many things, you will have to follow your instincts and give an agency a try. Then you have real experience to act on – you can always change agents.

A really good agent will suggest your name for jobs that your abilities will suit, and will help you get auditions and find work, but many will simply list you and leave it to clients to listen to demos and pick a talent. However it is better than being a sole individual as the agent usually advertises themselves and promotes a pool of talent which draws in producers who need to book a voice.

What can you do to promote yourself?

Even if you find a really good agent and they take you on, there is a lot you can do to maximize your chances of working.

Your aim is to become known to clients and to have them listen to your demo. Create a postcard that is simple, memorable and inexpensive. It doesn't have to be glossy and in three colours which makes it expensive to print.

Create a mailing list. You can find out what clients exist in the sectors of the industry you are interested in by checking the internet, the yellow pages, industry magazines and asking your agent.

If you want work reading audio books check out the covers of audio books being sold in the marketplace and note the production companies.

Try to keep an updated list of the names of people who hire voice-over talent, rather than just send your card to no specific person in the company. A telephone call to a company can produce this information. If you mail a card every four months or so, you are putting your name and skill areas in front of producers, and reminding them that you are available. Even if you have worked for a client in the past you can't count on being asked again and must prompt their memories.

If you can afford it, send a copy of your demo CD with your postcard and your C.V. If your agent has a master CD with samples of all the voices with their agency, note the track number of your voice and send postcards to potential clients suggesting they check out that track. When clients receive agency master CD's they do not sit down and go through them eagerly when they arrive – but if they are in need of talent for a job they will reach for the CD and listen to some voices. If they are already familiar with your name, they are that much more likely to listen to your track. You increase the chances of being booked.

Don't make phone calls to promote yourself – though some people do. In my experience this is seen as a nuisance by busy people, and will have you remembered for the wrong reasons.

Should you call your agent regularly?

This has to be managed with care. It is simply demoralising for you both, if their only response to a weekly call is "Sorry, there's nothing for you, yes, we'll definitely call you if something comes up". They too are busy, hopefully answering calls from clients seeking talent, not uselessly reassuring you that you're not forgotten. Again you don't want to be an irritation. However, if you can find a diplomatic excuse for calling occasionally, such as to ask a question, it may be to your advantage.

Media producers and casting directors do sometimes describe the voice or feel that they are looking for and ask for suggestions. A good agent will offer a few appropriate names; they won't ruin the long term relationship by suggesting random names on their books, but they may suggest your name if you're suitable and you've recently crossed their minds.

Even a new and inexperienced talent may be suggested. An agent can be helpful to both a client and a voice talent and say "Jane Smith is a fresh voice and new to the industry but she's keen". This manages client expectations if Jane is a bit nervous! So keeping your name and vocal strengths in your agent's mind is sensible, especially if the agency has a lot of names on its books. So keep in touch but not too much!

Promoting yourself on the web

You are your own business, and as any business textbook will tell you, advertising and marketing is vital. You can increase your visibility and the chances of being booked by creating your own website, or subscribing to an online service which will set up a webpage for you. It enables you to provide more samples of your voice and give a bit more information on your experience. Of course good word of mouth about your talent and pleasant professionalism is the very best form of advertising.

How do you build your own website?

There are short courses available and how-to-do-it books. Many senior students with IT skills are competent enough to set up a simple website. However it isn't just a matter of the technical know-how. A website must communicate well. Look at other websites and notice what works and what doesn't. Too many words and visual clutter do not give a good impression. Sometimes paying a professional to create and manage a website can be a better option. You will find plenty of webmaster services on the web. Managing a website involves ensuring a website has a registered domain name which is renewed when required, updating the look occasionally, and technical support if needed. These services will cost of course.

If you think setting up your own site is practical for you, the first thing to do is register your domain name. It might be your name, but you still need to check and see if that name is available, and purchase the right to use it as a web address. Go to http://www.register.com or to http://www.networksolutions.com. You will be able to see if your preferred name is available. Once you have purchased the right to use it, you have reserved it and then you can take your time setting up your website, or finding an internet website company to host your site.

Using an Online Marketplace

The web also offers "online marketplaces" where clients can post a job and voice talents can offer their services and send a sample of their voice. If chosen, the voice talent will record the script, usually in their home studio, and deliver the finished recording to the client remotely by email or FTP (File Transfer Protocol – used for delivering large files such as .wav or .aiff).

These marketplace sites can be a good resource for finding work. Check out www.voices.com, www.bodalgo.com or www.voice123.com. All of these marketplaces are leaders in the field and offer several auditions each week, often three or four every day. They charge around £200 per year to be able to audition, and they do not take any commission from your earnings. You can get listed on these sites for free, however, you will not be invited to audition for any jobs available. Although you may not receive invitations to audition, you are still visible on the site as a registered voice artist, clients will find you, they will be able to listen to your demos, and if you are suitable, they can contact you direct. So even if funds are currently low and a full membership is outside of your budget, it's still worth registering for a free listing.

Other freelancer sites

There are a few other sites that I recommend where beginners to the voice-over industry can find work.

Although the voice-over marketplaces are an excellent resource and give the opportunity to audition for several jobs every week, you must not forget that the majority of talent registered, are professional voice-over talent who have years of experience. It's tough competition and can be quite deflating if you audition for 30, 40, 50 jobs or more and don't even get a sniff of interest. That's often because, for each job advertised, there may be 40 or 50 other talents auditioning for the same job, most with more experience than you have.

For a complete beginner I recommend registering with www.Elance.com, www.Freelancer.com and www.Vworker.com. All of these sites have thousands of jobs available every day, a small percentage of these jobs are for voice talent, where you can usually audition for at least 4 or 5 jobs per week. The competition is much less and you are likely to be hired much more frequently.

The jobs advertised on these sites usually have lower budgets than the voice-over marketplaces, which is ideal for a beginner. You can start with low budget work, get lots of experience and a good number of clients under your belt, before making the move to the more competitive arenas of Voices.com or Voice123.com

All of these sites have a basic free membership which allows you to bid for up to 20 or 30 jobs every month, which is more than adequate. If you want to upgrade, it will cost you a monthly fee. For example, an upgrade on Elance will cost $10 USD per month (about £6 GBP). You will in effect, be buying more bids, however, this is not necessary to begin with.

When you are awarded work through these sites, you will have to pay a commission to the site, which is usually deducted from your bid amount. Commissions average between 8.75% on Elance to 15% on Vworker, so remember to build this commission in to your proposal before you bid.

Social Networking

In the last 5 years, there has been an explosion in social networking. These days, you are a nobody if you don't have a Facebook, LinkedIn or a Twitter account. You only have to watch the TV ads to find directions to the Facebook accounts of major companies such as Coka-Cola, L'oreal, Vogue and most other high profile companies. If you want to be recognised as a professional voice-over artist, register for an account with Facebook, Twitter and LinkedIn.

These social networking sites and a valuable resource in connecting with other people in the industry and in related industries, such as publishing and media production, and it's not uncommon to be offered work through your social network connections.

It is worth remembering that just having an account with Facebook or LinkedIn, is not enough, you need to keep it updated, even if it's only one a week. The more often people see your updates, the more likely it is that they will remember you when they need to hire a voice-over artist.

It's also worth subscribing to discussion groups, forums and blogs. Post to them regularly. Your name will soon get recognised and potential customers will start to take an interest.

Chapter 10

Auditioning for work

Auditioning or bidding for your first voice-over jobs can be a very daunting and sometimes, frightening experience. Even the most seasoned actors and voice over performers suffer from nerves at an audition. This is quite normal and shouldn't put you off.

The most important thing to remember is, not to lie about your experience or qualifications. If you do, the customer will have very high expectations, especially with regard to turnaround times and 'getting it right first time'. It's always best to be honest, this way you won't let your customer down or give them the any false impressions. Explain that you are new to the industry, but you are extremely keen to provide a professional result.

Example cover letter for new voice talent

Dear xxx

I would like to audition for the voice over project advertised. Despite being reasonably new to the industry, I am very conscientious, reliable and eager to make a good impression.

Although I currently have limited experience, I am able to carry out your project in a professional manner, and I am confident that I can provide the recording to meet your standards and requirements.

I have attached my voice-reel demo for your consideration. I recommend a visit to www.website.com where you will find a short biography and further voice samples.

I welcome the opportunity of working with you on this project, and look forward to being a part of your success.

Kind Regards

Jane Smith

www.janesmith.com
info@janemith.com
Tel: 01234 567 890

Don't expect to be hired right away with your first audition, although it does happen quite often, especially if your voice is a perfect fit for what the customer had in mind. Most clients (especially those hiring from the freelancer sites) are quite willing to hire new talent and will be more than happy to give you a chance.

If you are lucky enough to be selected to read a custom audition (record a part of the actual script), or even awarded the work. Be sure to thank the client straight away and let them know that you won't let them down.

If a customer has requested that you record a custom audition, treat it as if you had already been awarded the job and make it as professional as you possibly can. Use the same equipment and software that you would use if you were actually recording the finished product. For instance, don't use the built in microphone on your lap top because you're currently away from your PC or studio, most customers are reasonably patient and would prefer a good, professional sounding sample to something that was recorded in a hurry.

Setting your rates

This is one of the most discussed subjects among voice-over talent. Everyone seems to have a different fee structure and there are no set industry standard rates or minimum fees. If you are a member of one of the performing arts unions, such as Equity in the UK, they do have set minimum rates for specific projects. However, I don't recommend joining a performing arts union until you have a lot of experience and several clients under your belt.

In the meantime, how much do you charge as a freelance voice artist who is new to the industry?

If you audition for a project that states a maximum budget of $500, it does not mean that the client is willing to pay $500, it usually means that if they can find a suitable voice talent who can complete the project for $300 and that artist fits all the customers other requirements, then that's the one that will probably be hired.

Customers fall in to two categories; the "quality conscious" and the "budget conscious". A customer who is more concerned with the quality of the finished product than the cost, will usually opt for a talent in the mid to top end of their budget range, sometimes they will even go over budget for the right voice.

The budget conscious customer will hire the voice artist that quotes the lowest or near lowest fee, who closely resembles that which they were looking for, in terms of accent or dialect, gender, age range etc.

How do you tell which is which? A lot of information can be gathered from the actual job posting, for instance, if a customer states "this should be an easy job for someone who knows what they are doing" or "shouldn't take more than 10 minutes of your time", more often than not, they have a low budget. Most people outside of the industry are completely unaware of the amount of time and work that goes in to a finished voice-over, not to mention the training, marketing and other expenses that we have. They presume that a five minute finished voice over should take no more than ten minutes. They couldn't be more wrong.

You can also usually tell if a customer is willing to pay a little more for the right voice (quality conscious) by the wording that they use in the job description. If they refer to tone, pitch, pace, voice direction, format or anything technical relating to the recording and editing process, then it is obvious that they have some idea what they are talking about, so it usually follows that they will know what kind of quotes to expect.

As a beginner, you're unlikely to be hired for the big budget jobs right away, unless you can display exceptional talent and ability with your demos. The best course of action for a beginner, in any field, is to start at the bottom and work up.

Even starting at the bottom with very low budget work, can still earn you the equivalent of £20 or £30 an hour, which is not to be sniffed at. However, don't be under the impression that you will be working for ten, twenty or even thirty hours a week at that rate, voice-over work can be very inconsistent. One week you may only work for one or two hours, other weeks you could work for ten or twenty hours, for instance, recording an audio book, or several small jobs for different clients.

When you quote for your first jobs on the freelancer sites like Elance, a good starting rate for up to one or two minutes of finished voice over would be around $50 (about £28). If the customer states a word count for the script, rather than a finished audio time, work on the basis that there is somewhere in the region of 150 to 180 words per minute.

For larger jobs, e.g. anything more than ten to fifteen minutes of finished voice over (over 1000 words), quote in the region of $150 to $200 (£85 to £125) for the first 1000 words and a few cents per word over and above 1000. For example, if a script is 1300 words, my advice would be to quote around $150 for the first 1000 words and say 10 cents per extra word, therefore, your quote for this project would be:

First 1000 words	-	$ 150.00
300 words @ $0.10 per word	-	$ 30.00
Total	-	$ 180.00

When you start applying for long form narration work such as audio books or anything with a finished audio time (recorded and fully edited) of one hour or more, charge by the finished hour, for example, first finished hour (around 10,000 words) $400, and $200 per finished hour over and above one hour. Using this method, a short audio book lasting three hours (about 30,000 words) would work out at $800. That equates to approximately £500 and would probably take a beginner eleven or twelve hours to complete, which means you've earned at least £40 per hour worked.

It's worth remembering that most jobs will be advertised in US Dollars, (USD or $), so it's a good idea to add a currency converter to your internet favourites list.

As you gain more experience and can display some good feedback from previous work, you can start to increase your rates. A more experienced voice over artist with a good reputation and great feedback, can regularly earn well in excess of £100 per hour.

Chapter 11
Practice Scripts

Commercials

Somerset Hills Real Estate:

Getting that big promotion must feel good. Why not celebrate moving up by moving to Somerset Hills? The neighbourhoods of Somerset Hills are now entering into their third phase of building! Choose from dozens of family homes on large plots tucked away on Lilies Fair Court, perfect for young families and parents who want a safe and secluded street on which to raise their kids. With homes selling quickly, you'd better act now so that you can move into your dream home before the first snowfall! Open houses are being held every Saturday and Sunday from 12 until 4. Somerset Hills: move in today and stay for a lifetime.

Green Gables:

You've always wanted to retire in style. The residents of Green Gables Retirement Community enjoy 25% more life and easy living! There's no need to cut the lawn, shovel the driveway, or climb unnecessary stairs. Those are just three great benefits of living at Green Gables. Green Gables, the world at your doorstep with all the amenities!

Adventure Travel:

(Inner monologue) Back to the old to do list again. Let's see… Climb Mount Everest… done. Snorkeling with the dolphins off the coast of Australia? Done. Sky diving in Borneo… yup, that's checked off too. Barreling over Niagara Falls (chuckle) – Nah, too risky! How about discovering a Land of Lost Caverns in the highlands of Costa Rica? (Reading) Easily trek to view scenic wonders of beauty and mystery… ancient unexplored caverns await… (Said to another person) Hey Alice, what do you think of this? (Announcer) Why just travel when you can 'adventure' travel? Call us today to book your next out-of-this-world thrill seeker vacation.

Honeymooners:

When you plan your honeymoon, don't just book the first flight to Tahiti… surprise your beloved with an unforgettably romantic getaway to one of the great European capital cities. Experience the finest that Paris, Rome, Madrid, and Athens have to offer… adorn your memories with haute cuisine, signature hotels, distinct cultures, and breathtaking wonders found only in continental Europe. Treat your New wife / husband to an Old World romance. Start your married life off right by honeymooning in style across the pond.

Va-Voom Shampoo:

Has your hair lost its lustre? Missing its bounce? Need some Va-va-va-voom? Let me tell you about this new shampoo I've been using. It's not like your ordinary, run of the mill, "I share this with my husband" shampoo - no, this one goes beyond the call of duty to tame frizzies, banish split ends and most importantly, it gives you the confidence you need (and a little bit of va-va-va-voooom!). Why use your old shampoo when you can experience the power and endurance of Va-Va-Va-Voom shampoo? Call or click for your free sample today.

Nocturnal Rest:

Maybe it's the way the sun kisses his skin or maybe it's the gentle shoulder rubs before bedtime. It could be the homemade Fettuccine Alfredo prepared last night, or perhaps it's the load of laundry you found neatly folded on the landing. Maybe it's just because he's there. Those actions say so much, even when words are hard to find. Let him know how much you love and appreciate him with a double decker grill, a large plasma TV, and let him renovate the basement into a sports bar... For those night's when you just can't get to sleep, try Nocturnal Rest and get to sleep... fast!

Scotts Surf Shop:

Ready for some fun in the sun? Not without our oversized beach towels! Scott's Surf Shop has everything to cover you at the beach, including swimming apparel, sun block, scuba gear, flip flops, and oversized beach towels made with shake-away technology that makes sure you leave the beach at the beach. Before you drive to the cottage, stop by Scott's Surf Shop to start your summer off right.

Investment Services:

Still hiding money under your mattress? Contrary to popular belief, investing your financial assets in a government savings bond can help your money grow! Our team of professionals at Global Transact House and Home will raise and nurture your investments as if they were their very own. We're very protective of our young! Trust our experts to take care of your hard-earned money and make it work for you.

Agilent

Man has always dreamed of getting to the other side. Some make it, some don't. But at least your phone calls get there. Because Agilent provides technologies for almost every kind of communications network. From way down here to way up here.

Expedia

Whatever you're looking for in a vacation, you can find it at Expedia. Maybe it's a romantic trip to Paris or a cultural trip to New York. However you want to put it all together, Expedia can help you create the trip that's right for you.

IBM

To stay competitive, you're constantly searching for better ways to orchestrate the flow of information. How do you get more out of your PC's? How can you make the most of your existing systems? What can be done to streamline your organization? More often than not, the answer is IBM Client/Server. For more and more companies, IBM Client/Server is the key to getting everyone working in concert. We've done it for hundreds of companies…we can do it for you. IBM.

Men's Health

At point A, you're born. At point B, you're history. What happens in between is up to you. Live longer-and better-with Men's Health.

Pioneer Electronics

Some people just can't live without their subwoofers. Especially when they're equipped with our exclusive Voice Coil Cooling System technology. It lets our VCCS Subs handle up to 800 watts of power while producing clear, accurate and most importantly, loud bass. It's the kind of sound you can't do without. Under any circumstances. PIONEER. Everything else comes second.

Flaming Salsa

I was fed up with products claiming they were "Insanely Spicy," or "Extra Extra Hot!" until I tried new Flaming Salsa. IT'S HOT!! Flaming hot.

Godiva Chocolate

Now Everyone Can Get To Heaven. Perhaps you've sinned once or twice. But when you indulge in the luscious richness of our delectable milk chocolate truffles, you too will experience your own little moment in heaven.

Spirituality.com

Balance: We're always striving for harmony between our careers, our relationships, our bodies and our minds. And often, we exhaust our emotional resources trying. Perhaps the answer lies in finding a new source of guidance and inspiration; a source of fresh perspectives on everyday life; a source like spirituality.com. A different kind of on-line search. Spirituality.com

Starbucks

Look for Starbucks coffee in a grocery store near you then sit back and enjoy the exceptional taste of Starbucks at home.

Station Imaging

Extreme sports network:

Ever wanted to know what it's like to go flying through the air on a dirt bike - for a living? Watch our series chronicling the journey of one man, one bike, and candid interviews with some of his paramedic friends, tonight on the Extreme Summer Sports Network.

Almost the end of the biking hour... Surfs up, dude! Join Chris, Damon, and Matt as they ride the waves of Waimea Bay during the Big Wave Season. It's here! Hang out with the gang, right after Dirt Biking, tonight on the Extreme Summer Sports Network.

Fashionista TV:

To be a one of today's top models, you need poise, beauty, and that elusive 'Je ne sais quoi'. Do you have what it takes? Find out on Wednesday's episode of "So, you wanna be a supermodel", only on Fashionista TV. Call your local cable provider for more information.

Think you're cut from the same cloth as Cindy, Tyra, or Halle? Enter our contest online to win a free trip for two to London to live the high life! Not only will you stay in the finest hotels, eat the most exquisite food, and enjoy a sublime nightlife, you'll get to strut your stuff on the catwalk and hobnob with the fashion elite.

Evening News:

Exclusive reports on the state of the nation, climbing gas prices, and the national childcare program, all coming up tonight on your evening news.

Parents everywhere are dying to get their hands on one of these. No, it's not a Tickle Me Elmo doll... it's a handheld digital dictionary! Find out why kids are going high tech and how their pocket computers may spell the end for conventional learning, tonight on the news at six.

Current UK

You're listening to 91.7 FM Current UK. News, views and opinions from the guy down the street, He knows it all!

Hard Rock Radio

Don't move! Stay right where you are! ... and sing along to your favourite all time rock classics. Hard Rock Radio. Worth doing time for!

Telephone System Recordings

Abigail Jane's Flowers:

Thank you for calling Abigail Jane's Flowers, your friendly neighbourhood florist for weddings and all of your special occasions.

To speak with a floral consultant, press 1

To place an order, press 2

To speak with Genevieve Thompson in arranging, press 3

To speak with Abigail Jane Frailey, press 4

To leave a message in the company mail box, press 5

Grimsby Developments:

Thank you for calling Grimsby Developments, the leader in heritage home development. All of our lines are busy, so please leave your name, contact number, and a brief message, a representative will return your call as soon as they can. Thank you, and have a nice day.

Unavailable:

I'm sorry. The extension you have dialed is unavailable. Press 5 to leave a message now.

Incorrect:

I'm sorry, you have pressed an incorrect key. Please try again, or press 3 to return to the main menu.

Ace BC Electrical:

Thank you for holding, your call is very important to us and will be answered shortly. Don't forget to ask our representative about the special Christmas discounts currently available in our electronics department, including a massive £100 saving on a Samsung 40 inch Full HD ten-eighty P LCD TV, now only £399! Please continue to hold.

Prompts:

Please hang up and try your call again. This is a recording. Please hang up and try your call again... (looping)

The number you are trying to reach is no longer in service. Please hang up and try your call again.

I'm sorry. The extension you have dialed is unavailable. Press 5 to leave a message now.

I'm sorry, you have pressed an incorrect key. Please try again, or press 3 to return to the main menu.

The number you have dialed is currently busy. If you would like us to notify you when the line is free, press 4 now.

Please enter your password.

You have 3 new messages. To listen to your messages, press one.

Educational Narration/Documentary

Elephants of Kilimanjaro:

A young elephant takes its first wobbly steps after birth in the heartland of Kilimanjaro, named after its majestic mountain, also the highest peak in all of Africa. This little elephant will enjoy all that the region has to offer, including semi-arid savannas and wetlands, growing up amidst several diverse ecosystems that connect the circle of life in Kilimanjaro.

Other inhabitants, great and small, of this beautiful heartland are lions, cheetahs, the striped hyena, giraffes, and an assortment of aviary creatures such as the eagle and hawk, all of which will influence the life of our little friend.

Treading carefully behind her mother, the young elephant learns to follow her elders, gaining a sense of safety and belonging. She is the newest member of her herd, and will someday establish herself as the leader of her own herd, but her time will come soon enough.

The Heart Of River Valley:

This lovely four bedroom home is nestled amongst rolling hills in the heart of the River Valley. Solid hardwood floors reminiscent of the Edwardian era grace all of the living space in the home, complete with original windows, doors, and heating grates, endowing the entire residence with a personality that you will not find anywhere else. The gracious dining room is adorned with crown mouldings and comes complete with french doors and a glorious chandelier that any hostess would be proud of. One of the greatest features is the newly updated kitchen with two sinks, ornate cabinetry, and a gourmet cooking area fit for the chef in the family. This home has 2 full baths and updated copper plumbing and wiring, a rare find for a home built in this era. Built on a mature treed lot, you will wake up to the songs of birds every morning, and settle down to the quiet sunset from the porch facing West each night. A finished basement, attic, and additional storage in the garage make this home the perfect fit for your family. Start a new life with the quality and assurance of the past. Inquire about this property today.

The fund for animals

In the 21st century, compassion is the new fashion. Be a real trend-setter and don't buy fur coats or fur trim. No matter how you look at it, fur isn't cool – it's cruel. The Fund for Animals. We speak for those who can't. www.fund.org.

Smoke Alarm

A smoke alarm can save your life but not if it's silent. Over 60% of fire fatalities and countless injuries happen where smoke alarms are installed but fail to work. Remember, only working smoke alarms save lives, so sound the alarm to your family and friends, a silent smoke alarm may be the last thing they never hear.

E-Learning

Search engine optimization:

One of the most important aspects of search engine optimization (SEO) is optimizing your page content. "Optimizing" simply means putting the keywords you've selected into your web pages in the right places, with the right formatting.

The first thing to understand is that you should only use 1 or 2 search terms to optimize each page. Once you've selected a page to optimize, and the search terms you are going to use, all you have to do is put those words in the right places of the HTML code and you're done.

Where the search terms go:

1. Your page's title tag

2. Your "keywords" and "description" META tags

3. In the first paragraph of body text

4. In the text of any links that point to the page

If you need ideas for words that you can use to describe your services, view our list of keywords.

Computer Terminology:

Access time - The performance of a hard drive or other storage device – how long it takes to locate a file.

Active program or window - The application or window at the front (foreground) on the monitor.

Alias - an icon that points to a file, folder or application.

Alert (alert box) - a message that appears on screen, usually to tell you something went wrong.

Audio Books (Fiction)

Frankenstein:

It was on a dreary night of November that I beheld the accomplishment of my toils. With an anxiety that almost amounted to agony, I collected the instruments of life around me, that I might infuse a spark of being into the lifeless thing that lay at my feet.

It was already one in the morning; the rain pattered dismally against the panes, and my candle was nearly burnt out, when, by the glimmer of the half-extinguished light, I saw the dull yellow eye of the creature open; it breathed hard, and a convulsive motion agitated its limbs.

How can I describe my emotions at this catastrophe, or how delineate the wretch whom with such infinite pains and care I had endeavored to form? His limbs were in proportion, and I had selected his features as beautiful. Beautiful! Great God! His yellow skin scarcely covered the work of muscles and arteries beneath; his hair was of a lustrous black, and flowing; his teeth of a pearly whiteness; but these luxuriances only formed a more horrid contrast with his watery eyes, that seemed almost of the same color as the dun-white sockets in which they were set, his shriveled complexion and straight black lips.

King Lear:

Rumble thy bellyful! Spit, fire! spout, rain!

Nor rain, wind, thunder, fire are my daughters.

I tax not you, you elements, with unkindness.

I never gave you kingdom, call'd you children,

You owe me no subscription. Then let fall

Your horrible pleasure. Here I stand your slave,

A poor, infirm, weak, and despis'd old man.

But yet I call you servile ministers,

That will with two pernicious daughters join

Your high-engender'd battles 'gainst a head

So old and white as this! O! O! 'tis foul!

Treasure Island:

The appearance of the island when I came on deck next
morning was altogether changed. Although the breeze had now
utterly ceased, we had made a great deal of way during the
night and were now lying becalmed about half a mile to the
south-east of the low eastern coast. Grey-colored woods
covered a large part of the surface. This even tint was indeed
broken up by streaks of yellow sand-break in the lower lands,
and by many tall trees of the pine family, out-topping the
others--some singly, some in clumps; but the general coloring

was uniform and sad. The hills ran up clear above the vegetation in spires of naked rock. All were strangely shaped, and the Spy-glass, which was by three or four hundred feet the tallest on the island, was likewise the strangest in configuration, running up sheer from almost every side and then suddenly cut off at the top like a pedestal to put a statue on.

Pride And Prejudice:

"You are too sensible a girl, Lizzy, to fall in love merely because you are warned against it; and, therefore, I am not afraid of speaking openly. Seriously, I would have you be on your guard. Do not involve yourself or endeavor to involve him in an affection which the want of fortune would make so very imprudent. I have nothing to say against him; he is a most interesting young man; and if he had the fortune he ought to have, I should think you could not do better. But as it is, you must not let your fancy run away with you. You have sense, and we all expect you to use it. Your father would depend on your resolution and good conduct, I am sure. You must not disappoint your father."

"My dear aunt, this is being serious indeed."

"Yes, and I hope to engage you to be serious likewise."

Alice In Wonderland:

The Caterpillar and Alice looked at each other for some time in silence: at last the Caterpillar took the hookah out of its mouth, and addressed her in a languid, sleepy voice.

`Who are YOU?' said the Caterpillar.

This was not an encouraging opening for a conversation. Alice replied, rather shyly, `I-- I hardly know, sir, just at present-- at least I know who I WAS when I got up this morning, but I think I must have been changed several times since then.'

`What do you mean by that?' said the Caterpillar sternly. `Explain yourself!'

`I can't explain MYSELF, I'm afraid, sir' said Alice, `because I'm not myself, you see.'

`I don't see,' said the Caterpillar.

`I'm afraid I can't put it more clearly,' Alice replied very politely, `for I can't understand it myself to begin with; and being so many different sizes in a day is very confusing.'

`It isn't,' said the Caterpillar.

`Well, perhaps you haven't found it so yet,' said Alice; `but when you have to turn into a chrysalis--you will some day, you know--and then after that into a butterfly, I should think you'll feel it a little queer, won't you?'

`Not a bit,' said the Caterpillar.

`Well, perhaps your feelings may be different,' said Alice; `all I know is, it would feel very queer to ME.'

`You!' said the Caterpillar contemptuously. `Who are YOU?' Which brought them back again to the beginning of the conversation. Alice felt a little irritated at the Caterpillar's making such VERY short remarks, and she drew herself up and said, very gravely, `I think, you ought to tell me who YOU are, first.'

`Why?' said the Caterpillar.

Here was another puzzling question; and as Alice could not think of any good reason, and as the Caterpillar seemed to be in a VERY unpleasant state of mind, she turned away.

`Come back!' the Caterpillar called after her. `I've something important to say!'

Dracula

A great bat came flapping into the room. It drove the weird women away. Poor Renfield fell down, fainting from fright. In an instant, the bat disappeared. In its place was the smiling figure of Count Dracula! He was ready to claim his victim! Once bitten by the vampire, Renfield became Dracula's slave. The evil Count wanted to go to England. Coffins, filled with Transylvanian earth, were taken to a ship and loaded on board. One of the coffins contained something else as well as dirt. Renfield guarded it well. When the ship landed in England, the horrified people at the dock found that the entire crew was dead. Only Renfield, now a raving madman, was left alive.

The Invisible Man

So ends the story of the strange and evil experience of the Invisible Man. And if you would learn more of him you must go to a little inn near Port Stowe and talk to the landlord. The sign of the inn is an empty board save for a hat and boots, and the name is the title of this story. The landlord is a short and corpulent little man with a nose of cylindrical protrusion, wiry hair, and a sporadic rosiness of visage. Drink generously, and he will tell you generously of all the things that happened to him after the time, and of how the lawyers tried to do him out of the treasure found upon him.

Madame Bovary

They returned to Yonville along the river. The summer weather had reduced its flow and left uncovered the river walls and water steps of the gardens along its bank. It ran silently, swift and cold-looking; long fine grasses bent with the current, like masses of loose green hair streaming in its limpid depths. Here and there on the tip of a reed or on a water-lily pad a spidery-legged insect was poised or crawling. Sunbeams pierced the little blue air bubbles that kept forming and breaking on the ripples; branchless old willows mirrored their gray bark in the water in the distance the meadows seemed empty all around them.

The wind in the willows

"Ratty," said the Mole suddenly one bright summer morning, "if you please, I want to ask you a favour." The Rat was sitting on the river bank, singing a little song. He had just composed it himself, so he was very taken up with it, and would not pay proper attention to the Mole or anything else. Since early morning he had been swimming in the river, in company with his friends the ducks. And when the ducks stood on their heads suddenly, as ducks will, he would dive down and tickle their necks, just under where their chins would be if ducks had chins, 'til they were forced to come to the surface again in a hurry, spluttering and angry and shaking their feathers at him, for it is impossible to say quite all you feel when your head is underwater.

Peter Rabbit

Peter was sitting by himself. He looked poorly, and was dressed in a red cotton pocket-handkerchief. "Peter," -- said little Benjamin, in a whisper -- "who has got your clothes?" Peter replied -- "The scarecrow in Mr. McGregor's garden," and described how he had been chased about the garden, and had dropped his shoes and coat. Little Benjamin sat down beside his cousin, and assured him that Mr. McGregor had gone out in a gig, and Mrs. McGregor also; and certainly for the day, because she was wearing her best bonnet.

Recommended Resources

Downloads:

http://audacity.sourceforge.net/download/ Audacity recording and editing free software.

http://www.nch.com.au/wavepad/masters.html Wavepad recording and editing software.

http://www.freeplaymusic.com/ Royalty free music to use in your demos or productions (usage fees payable).

Tutorials:

http://www.transom.org/tools/editing_mixing/200404.audacity. html audacity user guide.

www.scribd.com/doc/8463893/How-to-Use-Audacity-Guide audacity user guide.

www.webjam.com/alcelearning/wavepad_tutorial Wavepad user guide.

Training:

www,greatbritishvoice.info Voice over workshop for beginners, based in West Yorkshire, UK. Taught by Sharon Brogden (the author).

www.internetvoicecoach.com internet based coaching for beginners and more experienced talent.

www.speaktoinfluence.com Online voice coaching from Susan Berkley.

Demo Production:

www.greatbritishvoice.co.uk Voice over brokerage and audio production company offering professional demo creation at reasonable prices.

Finding work:

www.gbvcoltd.com voice over brokerage specialising in British accents, membership only site. Promotes members on and off the internet. Membership by audition only.

www.elance.com Freelancer website with a section especially for multimedia. Twenty bids per month free, monthly upgrade $9.99 (about £6.00) *www.freelancer.com* Freelancer website with lower budget projects and a section for audio services. (20 free bids per month, 10% commission charged on each awarded project).

www.VWorker.com Lower budget freelancer website with a section for multimedia. Free to bid, but 15% commission is charged on awarded projects.

www.guru.com Freelancer website, limited free bids per month, upgrade for unlimited bids. $74.95 quarterly (about £42.00)

www.voiceoverindex.com Voice over directory of international voice over artists offering a monthly listing with free royalty free music and SFX $5 USD per month. *RECOMMENDED.*

www.voices.com Dedicated online only, voice over marketplace. Free to register but to audition, upgrade is required. Several levels of membership starting at $20.00 per month (about £13.00). (preferred membership, annual rate)

www.voice123.com Dedicated online only, voice over marketplace. Free to register but to audition, upgrade is required.

Networking:

www.voiceover-casting.com New networking site for the voice over community.

www.voice-overs.com/forum Forum based site dedicated to the voice over community *www.voicepronetwork.com* Connect with beginners and professionals.

www.voiceoveruniverse.com website with resources, forums and chat areas.

www.LinkedIn.com Social networking site mainly business oriented.

www.Twitter.com Social networking site allowing short updates.

www.Facebook.com Social networking site (The largest at the time of writing).

Further Reading

All the following books can be found on Amazon.com

There's Money Where Your Mouth Is : An Insider's Guide to a Career in Voice-Overs.

Announcing.

Art of Voice Acting.

You Can Bank On Your Voice.

Speak To Influence:How To Unlock The Hidden Power of Your Voice

VO: Tales and Techniques of a Voice-Over Actor.

Talking Funny for Money : An Introduction to the Cartoon/Character/Looping Area of Voice-Overs.

Word of Mouth : A Guide to Commercial and Animation
Voice-Over Excellence.

How to Read Copy : Professionals Guide to Delivering Voice-
Overs and Broadcast Commercials/Book and Cassette.

Creating Character Voices for Fun & Profit.

Making Money in Voice-Overs.

Disclaimer

This publication is designed to provide competent and reliable information in regard to the subject matter covered. It is sold with the understanding that the author and publisher are not engaged in rendering legal, accounting or other professional advice. Laws and practices vary from country to country and from state to state. If legal advice or other expert assistance is required, the services of a competent professional should be sought. The author and publisher specifically disclaim any liability that is incurred from the use or application of the contents of this book.

4763957R00059

Printed in Great Britain
by Amazon.co.uk, Ltd.,
Marston Gate.